Leader's Guide for group study of

BE AVAILABLE

Warren W. Wiersbe

Leader's Guide prepared by
LIN JOHNSON

Eight Reproducible Response Sheets are included in a removable center section.

VICTOR BOOKS
A DIVISION OF SCRIPTURE PRESS PUBLICATIONS INC.
USA CANADA ENGLAND

Scripture quotations are taken from the *Holy Bible, New International Version®*. Copyright © 1973, 1978, 1984 by International Bible Society. Used by permission of Zondervan Publishing House. All rights reserved.

1 2 3 4 5 6 7 8 9 10   Printing/Year 98 97 96 95 94

ISBN: 1-56476-320-X
© 1994 by Victor Books/SP Publications, Inc.
All rights reserved.
Printed in the United States of America.

VICTOR BOOKS
A division of SP Publications, Inc.
1825 College Avenue, Wheaton, Illinois 60187

THE PLACE TO BEGIN

Before you start flipping through this Leader's Guide, stop for a couple of minutes and read pages 4–7. These pages will:
- Tell you what you'll need to know to prepare each lesson.
- Introduce different methods of leading group interaction.
- Help you evaluate how you're doing as a group leader.

KNOW YOUR GROUP

Picture the individuals who make up your group. What do you know about them? What do you need to know to lead them effectively? Here are a few suggestions:
- Develop warm relationships — get to know group members by name. Find ways to help members get to know each other as well.
- Find out what your group members already know and what they would like to know.
- Be a good listener.
- Promote an attitude of acceptance and respect among group members.

GET READY TO LEAD

If you are a little unsure of yourself because you're leading a group of adults for the first time, then follow the LESSON PLAN outlines for each session.

Using the guided discovery learning approach, each chapter will contain at least three sections:

- *Launching the Lesson* — activities that begin focusing on group members' needs.
- *Discovering God's Principles* — creative ways to communicate Bible truth.
- *Applying the Truth* — application activities that relate Bible truth to everyday life.

Some sessions may contain additional, optional sections such as:
- *Building the Body* — icebreakers and activities to help group members build relationships.
- *Prayer Time* — suggestions for praying together as a group.

REMEMBER THE BASICS

Read the entire text and this Leader's Guide. Underline important passages in the text and make notes as ideas come to you. Note any activities in the guide that take advance planning or preparation.

Follow these steps in planning each session:
- Make a brief outline of your lesson plan.
- Formulate and *write down* all the discussion questions you intend to use.
- Note all activities and interaction methods you plan to implement.
- Gather all the materials you will need for the session.

Each session should focus on at least one, and often several, Bible truths that can be applied directly to the lives of your group members. Encourage group members to bring their Bibles to each session and use them. It's also a good idea to have several modern-speech translations on hand for the purpose of comparison.

USE A VARIETY OF INTERACTION METHODS

Response Sheets
Several Response Sheets are provided for you in the removable center section of this guide. Response Sheets are designed to extend the lesson's impact.

The Response Sheets in this guide will help you enliven your sessions and encourage group involvement. They are numbered consecutively (Response Sheet 1—Response Sheet 8) and show with what sessions they should be used. The guide gives specific directions for when and how to use each Response Sheet in the lesson material.

Brainstorming
Announce the question or topic to be "stormed." Group members may make as many spontaneous suggestions as possible, not waiting to be called on. Don't allow anyone to criticize the suggestions. List suggestions on a chalkboard or poster board; when all are in, have the class evaluate the ideas. This method loosens up the group, involves nonparticipants, and produces new insights.

Group Bible Study
Each person should have her or his Bible open. Ask questions that will help the group learn what the passage you are studying says. Encourage sharing of insights as the group discusses the interpretations of the passage and its application to current needs. Always

summarize findings. This method makes group members think; it shows them how to study the Bible on their own and it increases participation and involvement.

Discovery Groups
Divide the group into small groups of three to six persons. Appoint a leader for each group or let groups select their own leaders. Assign a topic to each group. Several—or all—groups may discuss the same topic if necessary. Allow 5–8 minutes for discussion in the groups, then reconvene and get reports from group leaders. Jot findings on a chalkboard or poster board for discussion. Since many persons are freer to express themselves in small groups, this method provides maximum participation opportunity.

Role Play
Two or more group members, without advance notice or written scripts, act out a situation or relationship. Give them directions as to the kind of people they are to represent and the situation in which they find themselves. They speak extemporaneously. This method helps people "feel" situations, gives them opportunity to try different solutions, and creates interest in the lesson.

Skit
Have members read the parts of a brief script that highlights a point, provokes discussion, or presents information. Skits provide sessions with stimulating variety.

Dyads
Like *Discovery Groups*, except that there are only two people, sitting next to each other, in each "group." (If a person is left out in the pairing off, assign him to one of the twosomes.) This method makes it easy for shy persons to participate.

Discussion
In discussion, members interact not only with the group leader but with one another. Usually discussion is started by the group leader's asking a question to which there is more than a single acceptable answer. A member will respond to a question, someone else may disagree with him, and a third person may have additional comments. The leader is responsible for starting the discussion, keeping it "on track" by asking leading questions as necessary, and summarizing it after contributions cease. If a discussion gets out of hand and rambles, much of its value is lost.

Here are a few guidelines for leading discussion:
■ Maintain a relaxed, informal atmosphere.

- Don't call on people by name to take part unless you are sure they are willing to do so.
- Give a person lots of time to answer a question. If necessary, restate the question casually and informally.
- Acknowledge any contribution, regardless of its merit.
- Don't correct or embarrass a person who gives a wrong answer. Thank him or her; then ask, "What do the rest of you think?"
- If someone monopolizes the discussion, say, "On the next question, let's hear from someone who hasn't spoken yet."
- If someone goes off on a tangent, wait for him or her to draw a breath, then say, "Thanks for those interesting comments. Now let's get back to . . ." and mention the subject under consideration, or ask or restate a question that will bring the discussion back on target.
- If someone asks a question, allow others in the group to give their answers before you give yours.

EVALUATE YOUR EFFECTIVENESS

After each session, ask yourself the following questions:

_____ How well did each group member understand the lesson goals?

_____ How many group members actually took part in the lesson?

_____ Could I use other interaction methods to increase group member interest and participation?

_____ Did I nurture personal relationships with my group members?

_____ How well did I prepare the lesson?

_____ How did group members react to me as a group leader?

_____ What do I need to do to become a better group leader?

INTRODUCTION

Even though the Book of Judges records historical events that occurred over 1600 years ago, the truths it teaches are contemporary. As the author of Judges emphasized, "In those days Israel had no king; everyone did as he saw fit" (17:6; 21:25). What an apt description of our society! Everyone is doing his own thing without regard to God's commands.

As you and your group members study this book, you will focus on the cycle Israel repeated throughout this time period: *disobedience* to God, *discipline* through bondage to their enemies, *despair* during which they cried out to God, and *deliverance* through a judge God raised up. You will discover that those judges were ordinary people with weaknesses and fears like ours. But when they allowed God to use them, they were able to accomplish great things.

Before planning your first session, skim the entire text and this leader's guide. Note the suggested resources for additional reading, and begin to gather them. Read *The Place to Begin* in this guide for help in leading a group. Then prepare each session with the big picture in mind.

Note that a number of sessions suggest dividing group members into smaller groups and appointing leaders. It is quicker to divide members by where they are sitting. But sometimes you may want to add some fun to this process by having them form groups by birth month, color of shoes or clothing, occupations, etc. Appoint leaders in a similar way: the one wearing the most red, the one with the next birthday, the one with the largest shoe size, etc.

As the group leader, set an example by applying the biblical principles both before and after teaching them. Schedule a few minutes before or after each session to encourage one another and to add accountability for following through on the assignments. In some sessions, time has been designated for doing this in the *Building the Body* section. Ask for reports, share victories, and pray about defeats. Be sure you participate too so that group members know you are growing along with them. This sharing will help everyone get to know each another better and be better equipped to pray for one another between sessions.

May God use this study to challenge you and your group members to be available to Him.

Session One

IT WAS THE WORST OF TIMES
Judges 1–2

TEXT, CHAPTER 1

Session Topic
God wants total obedience to Him.

Session Goals
1. To identify situations in which it is difficult to obey God.
2. To explore how the Israelites disobeyed God during the times of the judges and what happened as a result.
3. To select one way to obey God this week.

Materials Needed
√ Bible
√ Copies of *Be Available* for the group
√ Multiple copies of several colors of construction-paper sheets or smaller squares
√ Copies of Response Sheet 1
√ Pencils
√ Visual Sketch 1

Special Preparation
1. If possible, distribute copies of the textbook to group members prior to the first session. Ask them to read the preface and chapter 1.
2. To get the big picture, read through the entire Book of Judges—preferably in one or two sittings.
3. To gain historical perspective, read the appropriate sections of an Old Testament or Bible survey book, such as *Survey of the Old Testament* by Paul N. Benware (Moody) or *Talk thru the Bible* by Bruce Wilkinson and Kenneth Boa (Nelson).

4. Using an exhaustive concordance, look up the words *obey* and *disobey* in Scripture. List what you learn about this topic, and prepare to share your insights when appropriate.
5. Reproduce Visual Sketch 1 as a poster. Keep this poster to use throughout this study.

LESSON PLAN

Building the Body *(5–10 minutes)*

Before the session begins, put the construction paper on a table or chair near the door. As group members arrive, ask them to select a color that expresses their obedience to God and prepare to tell why they chose it. For example, a member might choose yellow because she finds it easy to obey God. Someone else might choose black or dark blue because he struggles to obey. After everyone has chosen a color, go around the circle and have each group member explain why he or she chose that color. Be sure you participate too.

Launching the Lesson *(5 minutes)*

Discuss: **When is it hard for believers to obey God? Why?** (For example, a group of coworkers invites a Christian who does not drink alcohol to join them for drinks after work. It's hard to decline the offer because the Christian doesn't want others to think he is too straight or not interested in being with them.)

Say: **The struggle with obedience to God is not new. In fact, it goes back to Adam and Eve. During this course, we're going to look at how the Israelites struggled with obedience during the 300-year period of the judges and what we can learn from them.**

Discovering God's Principles *(25–30 minutes)*

If your group studied the Book of Joshua from Warren Wiersbe's book *Be Strong*, ask one or more volunteers to review briefly that historical period. If not, summarize the background from the text and your reading in an Old Testament/Bible survey book.

Distribute copies of Response Sheet 1. Using this chart, survey the Book of Judges. Point out the space for group members to write personal applications. Encourage them to do so each week after the study.

Have group members read Joshua 24:23-31 and Judges 1:1–2:13. You may want to ask volunteers to read sections of these passages aloud. Then have group members contrast the end of Joshua with the beginning of Judges and account for the difference in the Israelites' attitude toward obeying God. Ask: **Why did Israel end up obeying her enemies instead of God?**

Ask someone to read Deuteronomy 7:1-5 aloud. Ask: **What was God's plan for the people of Israel when they entered the Promised Land? Why? How well did the Israelites obey this plan? What was the key to their victory over their enemies?** (Judges 1:19; cf. Rom. 8:31) **What happened when they failed to overtake their enemies?**

Have group members read Judges 2:11-23. Display Visual Sketch 1, showing Israel's cycles during the days of the judges. Ask members to match phrases from this passage with each step of the cycle. Mention that you will look at specific examples of this cycle as you proceed through the Book of Judges.

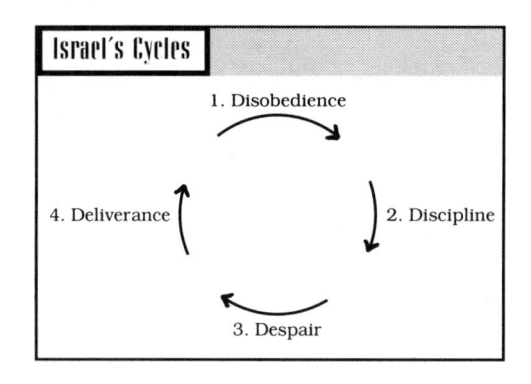

Israel's Cycles

1. Disobedience
2. Discipline
3. Despair
4. Deliverance

Visual Sketch 1
During the time period covered by the Book of Judges, Israel moved through a number of these cycles.

Ask: **How is contemporary society like the days of the judges? How is today's church like those times? What temptations do God's people face today that cause them to serve other gods? How can we avoid these temptations so we don't get caught in this type of cycle?**

Applying the Truth *(5–10 minutes)*

Discuss: **What did you learn about obedience and disobedience from this introduction to the times of the judges? What did you learn about God? How should this knowledge affect your attitude toward God's commands?**

Distribute pencils. Have everyone choose one way to obey God this week and write it in the fourth section of the Response Sheet chart under "Divine mercy."

Prayer Time *(5 minutes)*

Close with a few minutes of silent prayer. Encourage group members to talk with God about their attitudes toward God's commands and changes they need to make. Then close with audible prayer, affirming the group's desire to obey Him.

ASSIGNMENT

1. Instruct group members to read Judges 3 and chapter 2 of *Be Available* for the next session.
2. Encourage them to read the entire Book of Judges in one or two sittings to get the big picture and to memorize the key verse, Judges 17:6.
3. Have them think about resources they would want to have available if they were leading an army into battle.

Session Two

THE WEAPONS OF OUR WARFARE
Judges 3

TEXT, CHAPTER 2

Session Topic
God uses the resources we have to give us victory over our enemy Satan.

Session Goals
1. To identify the kinds of resources used in battles.
2. To discover how God used the resources Othniel, Ehud, and Shamgar had to gain victory over their enemies.
3. To identify resources we have that God can use for victory over Satan and to choose one to use this week.

Materials Needed
√ Bible
√ *Be Available*
√ Copies of Response Sheet 2
√ Pencils
√ Visual Sketch 1 poster
√ Chalkboard and chalk
√ Note cards

Special Preparation
1. Study 2 Corinthians 10:1-6 and Ephesians 6:10-20. You may want to consult commentaries on these passages, such as Warren Wiersbe's *Be Encouraged* and *Be Rich*. Brainstorm specific ways Satan tries to defeat us spiritually.
2. Using *Nave's Topical Bible* or *The Thompson Chain-Reference Bible,* study spiritual warfare. Be prepared to share some of your insights during the *Applying the Truth* segment.

3. If possible, skim *Battle Ready* by Mark R. Littleton (Victor Books) for suggestions on winning the war with temptation.

LESSON PLAN

Building the Body *(5 minutes)*

To encourage group members to grow spiritually by doing the assignments, ask a few volunteers to share how they obeyed God this past week and what happened as a result. Also ask for reports of how last session's study affected their attitudes toward obeying God throughout the week.

Launching the Lesson *(5 minutes)*

Ask: **If you were in charge of an army, what kind of resources would you want in order to win a battle? Why?** After taking a number of responses, remark on how appropriate they are. Then mention that when God equips His people for battling their enemies, He doesn't always use the most obvious resources—as you'll discover in Judges chapter 3.

Discovering God's Principles *(25–35 minutes)*

Say: **This chapter introduces us to the first three judges. Let's look at their lives and battles.** Distribute copies of Response Sheet 2 and pencils. Instruct half of the group to fill in the chart for Othniel and Shamgar and the other half, Ehud and Shamgar. After about 10 minutes, display Visual Sketch 1 which you created for the previous session. Call for reports about each judge, correlating the sections on the chart with the steps in this cycle. Encourage everyone to fill in the blank section of the sheet as answers are given.

Read this quote from page 26 of the text: "Charles Spurgeon said that God never allows His people to sin successfully. Their sin will either destroy them or it will invite the chastening hand of God." Ask: **How did the times of the judges illustrate the truth of this statement?**

Discuss the following questions:

- *What was God trying to teach the Israelites through these enemies?*
- *What resources did each of these judges have that God was able to use to gain victory over the enemy?*

- *What did you learn from the lives of these judges?*
- *Why did the people revert back to sin after the judge died?*

Applying the Truth *(10–15 minutes)*

Ask: **What enemies do we battle today? What forms do the battles take?**

After taking responses, have a couple of volunteers read 2 Corinthians 10:3-4 and Ephesians 6:10-12 aloud. Be sure everyone understands that we are battling an unseen enemy with greater power than the nations Israel fought against.

What resources do we have that God can use to defeat these enemies? How can He use each of them?

List responses on the chalkboard as they are given. Encourage group members to think beyond prayer, Scripture, and the Spirit without downplaying their importance. To help them broaden their thinking, remind them of Ehud's resource of strategy and Shamgar's resource of courage. Challenge the group with this quote from page 28 of the textbook: "Never underestimate the good that one person can do who is filled with the Spirit of God and obedient to the will of God."

Distribute note cards. Instruct everyone to list all the resources for victory over Satan and sin that they personally possess. Then have them circle one they know they can use this week.

Prayer Time *(5 minutes)*

Have everyone pair off and share the resources they circled and how they can use them. Instruct them to offer their lists of resources to God in prayer and pray for their partner's cooperation with God in gaining victory over Satan and his schemes this week.

ASSIGNMENT

1. Have group members read Judges 4 and 5 and chapter 3 of the text.
2. Encourage everyone to continue to pray for their partners throughout the week.
3. Ask group members to think about what kind of person God wants to use.

Session Three

"TWO ARE BETTER THAN ONE, AND THREE ARE BETTER STILL"
Judges 4–5

TEXT, CHAPTER 3

Session Topic
God uses individuals who are faithful, available, and trusting to accomplish His work.

Session Goals
1. To illustrate the kind of person God wants to recruit into His service.
2. To discover the kind of people God used in Judges 4 and 5.
3. To evaluate our usability for God's service and choose one area that needs to be changed.

Materials Needed
√ Bible
√ *Be Available*
√ Poster board
√ Marking pens
√ Visual Sketch 1 poster
√ Visual Sketch 2 poster
√ Note cards
√ Pencils

Special Preparation
1. Prepare Visual Sketch 2 on a sheet of poster board or a length or shelf paper. Or prepare to draw it on a chalkboard.
2. Evaluate your own usability for God's service. How faithful, available, and trusting are you? Spend extra time in prayer, talking with God about changes you need to make before you teach this session.

LESSON PLAN

Launching the Lesson *(15 minutes)*

Form groups of three to five, and appoint leaders. Give each group a sheet of poster board and marking pens. Instruct them to create a poster for the kind of individual God wants to recruit into His service. Tell them to work quickly and not to be concerned about details. Allow no longer than ten minutes. Then have the groups show their posters.

Say: **Let's see how our descriptions compare with people God recruited in Judges 4 and 5.**

Discovering God's Principles *(20–35 minutes)*

Have group members turn to Judges 4 and 5. Ask volunteers to read aloud the following sections: 4:1-3, 4:4-10, 4:11-16, 4:17-23, 5:1-12, 5:13-18, 5:19-23, 5:24-31.

Show Visual Sketch 1. Match phrases from the beginning of Judges 4 with the steps in the cycle. Then discuss the following questions:

- *What kind of person was Deborah?*
- *What kind of person was Barak?*
- *Why did God choose these two people to deliver Israel from her enemy?*
- *How did the tribes respond to the call to battle? Why?* (5:12-18)
- *How did God help the Israelites gain victory over Sisera and his army?* (4:11-16; 5:19-23)
- *What kind of person was Jael?* (4:17-24; 5:24-27)
- *How did God use her to clinch Israel's victory?* (4:17-24; 5:24-27)
- *What is significant about the fact that God used two women to help His people?* (Do not let responses to this question sidetrack the discussion into an argument about women in leadership. It is sufficient to note that God does use women to accomplish His work. In this situation, His use of Deborah and Jael also may indicate a lack of the right kind of men to do the jobs.)
- *Why was it appropriate for Deborah and Barak to sing a song in response to their victory?*
- *What stands out to you from this song? How does it differ from the Christian songs we sing?*

- *What have you learned about the kind of people God recruits into His service?* (Encourage a variety of answers, then use Visual Sketch 2 as one way to summarize the qualities God is looking for: Faithful, Available, Trusting.)
- *Based on this passage, how would you change your recruiting poster?*

God's Recruits
Faithful
Available
Trusting

Visual Sketch 2
When God looks for people to use in His service, He looks for believers who are FAT: **F**aithful, **A**vailable, and **T**rusting.

Applying the Truth *(5 minutes)*

Ask: **If you had been an Israelite in this time period, do you think God would have recruited you to deliver His people? Why or why not?**

What is one change you need to make in your life to be more usable for God's service? (Instead of taking spoken responses, distribute note cards and pencils. Instruct everyone to write down one change and ways to effect it.)

Prayer Time *(5 minutes)*

Have group members form triads, share the changes they selected, and pray for one another.

ASSIGNMENT

1. Assign Judges 6 and chapter 4 of *Be Available* as reading for the next session.
2. Encourage everyone to pray for their two partners during the week.
3. Suggest that group members look up the word *trust* in a concordance and/or word-study book. Ask them to be prepared to share what they learned about trusting God.

Session Four

GOD'S MAN IN MANASSEH
Judges 6

TEXT, CHAPTER 4

Session Topic
God wants us to trust Him no matter how bad the situation seems.

Session Goals
1. To describe our trust from God's point of view.
2. To explore Gideon's level of trust in God.
3. To evaluate our level of trust in God and take steps to increase it this week.

Materials Needed
√ Bible
√ *Be Available*
√ Note cards
√ Pencils
√ Visual Sketch 1 poster
√ Question sheets as described under "Special Preparation"
√ Copies of Response Sheet 3

Special Preparation
1. On separate sheets of paper, write each of these questions and Bible references:

   ■ Does God really care about us? Judges 6:1-13
   ■ Does God know what He's doing? Judges 6:14-24
   ■ Will God take care of me? Judges 6:25-32
   ■ Does God keep His promises? Judges 6:33-40

2. Reflect on how well you trust God, especially in bad situations.

Then write a description of your trust level in six words or less.
3. Using an exhaustive concordance and/or word-study book, look up the word *trust* to find out what Scripture says about trusting God. Plan to incorporate some of your discoveries when you teach.

LESSON PLAN

Building the Body   (5 minutes)

Ask group members to report their progress in becoming more usable for God. Have volunteers share the change they are working on, what they did this past week, and any results they have seen. Be sure that you participate too.

Launching the Lesson   (5–8 minutes)

Distribute note cards and pencils. Ask: **If God sent an angel to our group, how would he describe your trust level in six words or less?** Read the description you wrote for yourself to stimulate your group members' thinking. Instruct them to write their descriptions on the cards. After a couple of minutes, call for responses.

Say: **When God called Gideon to lead His people, He sent the angel of the Lord, who greeted him with a two-word description, "mighty warrior." Let's see why the angel used these words to describe Gideon.**

Discovering God's Principles   (20–30 minutes)

Display Visual Sketch 1. Then say: **Once again, Israel was moving through this familiar cycle. Keep it in mind as we study Gideon and four doubts that were obstacles to his trusting God.**

Divide the group into four study groups, and appoint leaders. Give each group a sheet of paper with one of the doubts. Instruct them to read the verses listed and answer the question, giving reasons for their answers. After about ten minutes, reassemble the group. Call for responses.

When people have finished discussing the doubts from *Special Preparation*, discuss the following questions:

- What kind of person was Gideon?
- What was ironic about the angel's description of him?

- *How much did Gideon trust God when He first called him? Why?*
- *What did Gideon learn about God?*
- *How did that knowledge help him trust God more and serve Him?*

If you have time, you may want to discuss Gideon's fleeces, using these questions:

- *Why did Gideon use this method to discern God's will?*
- *Was it appropriate? Why or why not?*
- *Should believers today use this method of discovering God's will? Why or why not?*

Ask group members who did the word study on *trust* to share some of their findings. Add what you learned from your study.

Read this quote from page 50 of the textbook: "It has often been said that 'God's commandments are God's enablements.' Once God has called and commissioned us, all we have to do is obey Him by faith; and He will do the rest." Ask group members if they agree or disagree and why.

Applying the Truth *(10–12 minutes)*

Ask: **If you were to mark a thermometer to indicate the level of Gideon's trust in the Lord, at what temperature would your mark be?** Where would you mark it for yourself? Instead of taking oral responses to the second question, distribute copies of Response Sheet 3. Have everyone shade the thermometer to the level of their current trust in God and answer the question under it. Discuss ways we can increase our trust in God. Then have everyone choose one area in which to trust God more, circle it on the Response Sheet, and list steps to take this week to increase trust in that area.

Prayer Time *(5 minutes)*

Have a few minutes of sentence prayers, encouraging group members to thank God for what they learned about trusting Him from Gideon's life and asking for His help to trust Him more in the areas they recorded on their sheets.

ASSIGNMENT

1. Have group members read Judges 7 and chapter 5 of *Be Available* for the next session.
2. Encourage everyone to post their Response Sheets in a visible place at home to remind them to follow through on their decisions.
3. Ask group members to bring a one- or two-sentence definition of *faith* to the next meeting.

Session Five

FAITH IS THE VICTORY
Judges 7

TEXT, CHAPTER 5

Session Topic
Believers are either overcome because of unbelief or overcomers because of their faith.

Session Goals
1. To identify obstacles to exercising faith in God.
2. To discover ways God tests, encourages, and honors faith.
3. To commit to exercising faith in God this week.

Materials Needed
√ Bible
√ *Be Available*
√ Old magazines with pictures
√ Copies of Response Sheet 4
√ Pencils
√ Chalkboard and chalk
√ Wastebasket or trash bag

Special Preparation
1. Read Hebrews 11. What do you learn about faith from this chapter? Write a definition in your own words.
2. "Faith is one of the most precious treasures a man can possibly possess. It is a pity that so few understand what the Bible teaches about it. Faith is often confused with presumption, optimism, determination, superstition, and imagination. Actually, it is simply *believing*.... Obviously faith honors God, while doubting His Word must insult and displease Him" *(Weekly Review)*. What does this quote add to your definition of faith?

LESSON PLAN

Building the Body *(5 minutes)*

Ask: **How has your level of trust in God increased? What kinds of temptation did you face this past week that threatened your trust? How did God help you through it?**

If group members are hesitant to respond, help them feel more comfortable by sharing your experiences first.

Launching the Lesson *(8–10 minutes)*

Give each group member a magazine, and place extras nearby. Say: **Who or what gets in the way of your faith in God? Tear out at least one picture or word to illustrate your answer.**

Direct group members to the extra magazines if they cannot find something in the ones they received. When everyone has an illustration, go around the circle and have each person show and tell about it, including yourself. Have them save their pictures for later in the session.

Say: **Gideon faced the same kinds of temptations as he began to deliver God's people from the Midianites. Let's see what happened.**

Discovering God's Principles *(30–40 minutes)*

Distribute pencils and copies of Response Sheet 4. Have group members work in pairs to complete the chart, explaining how, in specific ways, God tests, encourages, and honors faith. While they study, draw the same chart on the chalkboard. When everyone is finished, call for responses for the first two columns and write them on the board. After talking about the test of faith, discuss why God tests our faith. Then remind your group that "a faith that can't be tested can't be trusted" (Wiersbe, page 59). Ask volunteers to share personal examples from the column called Me.

Ask group members to define faith. Add any insights you gained from your study of Hebrews 11 that are not mentioned. Then write a one- or two-sentence definition.

Discuss the following questions:

- *What was Gideon like in Judges, chapter 6?*
- *How had he changed by the time we read about him in chapter 7?*

- *What made the difference?*
- *What was prophetic about the angel's description of Gideon as a "mighty warrior"?*
- *What have you learned about God from Gideon's experiences?*
- *What have you learned about faith from his experiences?*
- *How can our faith help us be overcomers instead of overcome by temptation?*

Applying the Truth *(7–10 minutes)*

Have someone read Hebrews 11:6 aloud. Brainstorm ways we can build our faith today, listing ideas on the chalkboard as they are suggested. Encourage group members to be specific and practical and to go beyond the pat answers of prayer and Bible study.

Place a wastebasket or trash bag in the center of the room. Have everyone get out their illustrations from the beginning of the session. Then instruct them to throw these away as a symbolic gesture that they will not let those things get in the way of exercising faith in God this week.

Prayer Time *(5 minutes)*

Ask three volunteers to close in prayer, thanking God for testing our faith, encouraging our faith, and honoring our faith in Him. Also have someone pray for God's help to exercise faith in Him this week.

ASSIGNMENT

1. Assign Judges 8 and chapter 6 of *Be Available* as reading for the next session.
2. Encourage group members to memorize Hebrews 11:6 and meditate on it during the week.
3. Ask group members to think about different ways people manifest pride and why we struggle with it so much.

Session Six

WIN THE WAR, LOSE THE VICTORY
Judges 8

TEXT, CHAPTER 6

Session Topic
Pride leads to spiritual decline even after a major spiritual victory.

Session Goals
1. To illustrate pride.
2. To find out how pride led to Gideon's downfall.
3. To write and follow God's prescription for curing pride.

Materials Needed
√ Bible
√ *Be Available*
√ Aluminum foil or modeling clay
√ Paper
√ Pencils
√ Copies of Response Sheet 5

Special Preparation
1. Using an exhaustive concordance, study the words *pride/proud* and *humility* in Scripture.
2. If possible, read chapter 10, "Choosing Humility over Pride" in *Choose Your Attitudes, Change Your Life* by Robert Jeffress (Victor Books).

LESSON PLAN

Launching the Lesson *(10–12 minutes)*

Give everyone about two feet of aluminum foil or a lump of modeling clay. Instruct them to tear or sculpt it into an object that represents pride. After a few minutes, have everyone show and briefly explain their objects. If your group is large, have them share in smaller groups.

Say: **Pride often gets in our way, especially after a major spiritual victory. Let's see how it affected Gideon after he defeated the Midianites.**

Discovering God's Principles *(25–35 minutes)*

Continue: **To find out, we're going to interview Gideon.** Ask for two volunteers to role play Gideon, and divide the rest of your group in half. Assign Judges 8:1-17 to one group and one volunteer and Judges 8:18-32 to the second group and and the other volunteer. Instruct the groups to read their verses and use *Be Available* as necessary to prepare questions for an interview with Gideon. Tell the groups to write questions to ask "Gideon" so that they can find out what happened after his victory over Israel's enemy. Point out that good questions cannot be answered with yes or no and should start with who, what, where, when, why, or how. The two volunteers should prepare to answer possible questions as though they were Gideon. Distribute paper and pencils for writing questions and making notes.

After about ten or fifteen minutes, conduct the interviews with Gideon. Then discuss these questions:

- *How did Gideon go from a great military leader to someone who led the people into idolatry?* (Ask a volunteer to read Proverbs 16:18 aloud.)
- *What object do you think Gideon would have sculpted at the beginning of our session? Why?*
- *How did Gideon's pride affect those around him?*

Applying the Truth *(8–10 minutes)*

Say: **Pride is a deadly sin that most of us struggle with. But we don't have to yield to it. God has given us antidotes in His Word. Let's see what they are.** Distribute copies of Response

Sheet 5. Have group members work individually, in pairs, or in triads to read the verses and write God's prescription for curing pride.

Ask a few volunteers to read their prescriptions. Then encourage everyone to take them during the week.

Prayer Time *(3–5 minutes)*

Have a couple of volunteers close the session with prayer, thanking God for what you learned from Gideon's example and for His prescription for curing pride.

If your group members know the song "Humble Thyself in the Sight of the Lord," sing it together.

ASSIGNMENT

1. Instruct group members to read Judges 9 and chapter 7 of *Be Available* for the next session.
2. Encourage them to read their prescriptions for pride at least once a day and to follow them.
3. Suggest that they memorize Proverbs 16:18.
4. Ask group members to look for ways that people reap what they sow.

God's discipline.
he saw fit" (21:25).

ipline
ers 3–16)

Disorder
(Chapters 17–21)

| Tola, Jair (10) | Jephthah (11:1–12:7) | Ibzan, Elon, Abdon (12:8-15) | Samson (13–16) | Religious Confusion (17–18) | Immorality (19) | Civil War (20–21) |

ss purposes only.

The First Three Judges

	Othniel
Sins	
Enemy	
Years of Bondage	
Prayer/Cry	
Years of Peace	
Reasons for Victory	

Response Sheet 2 Use with session 2 of *Be Available*.
© 1994 by SP Publications, Inc. Permission granted to purchaser to reproduce this Response Sh

In what areas of your life do you need to trust God more? List them below.

Circle the area in which you want to increase your trust this week. Then list specific steps to take in that direction.

God and Faith

GOD	Gideon
Tests Faith	
Encourages Faith	
Honors Faith	

Response Sheet 4 Use with session 5 of *Be Available*.
© 1994 by SP Publications, Inc. Permission granted to purchaser to reproduce this Response Sh

Address _____ Phone _____

℞

_____ God the Father

Refill **unlimited** times
☐ may substitute
☒ may not substitute

Leaders in Demand

Jephthah's Home Life

Jephthah's

My Home Life

My

Response Sheet 6 Use with session 8 of *Be Available*.
© 1994 by SP Publications, Inc. Permission granted to purchaser to reproduce this Response Sh

Man
Judges 14:1-20

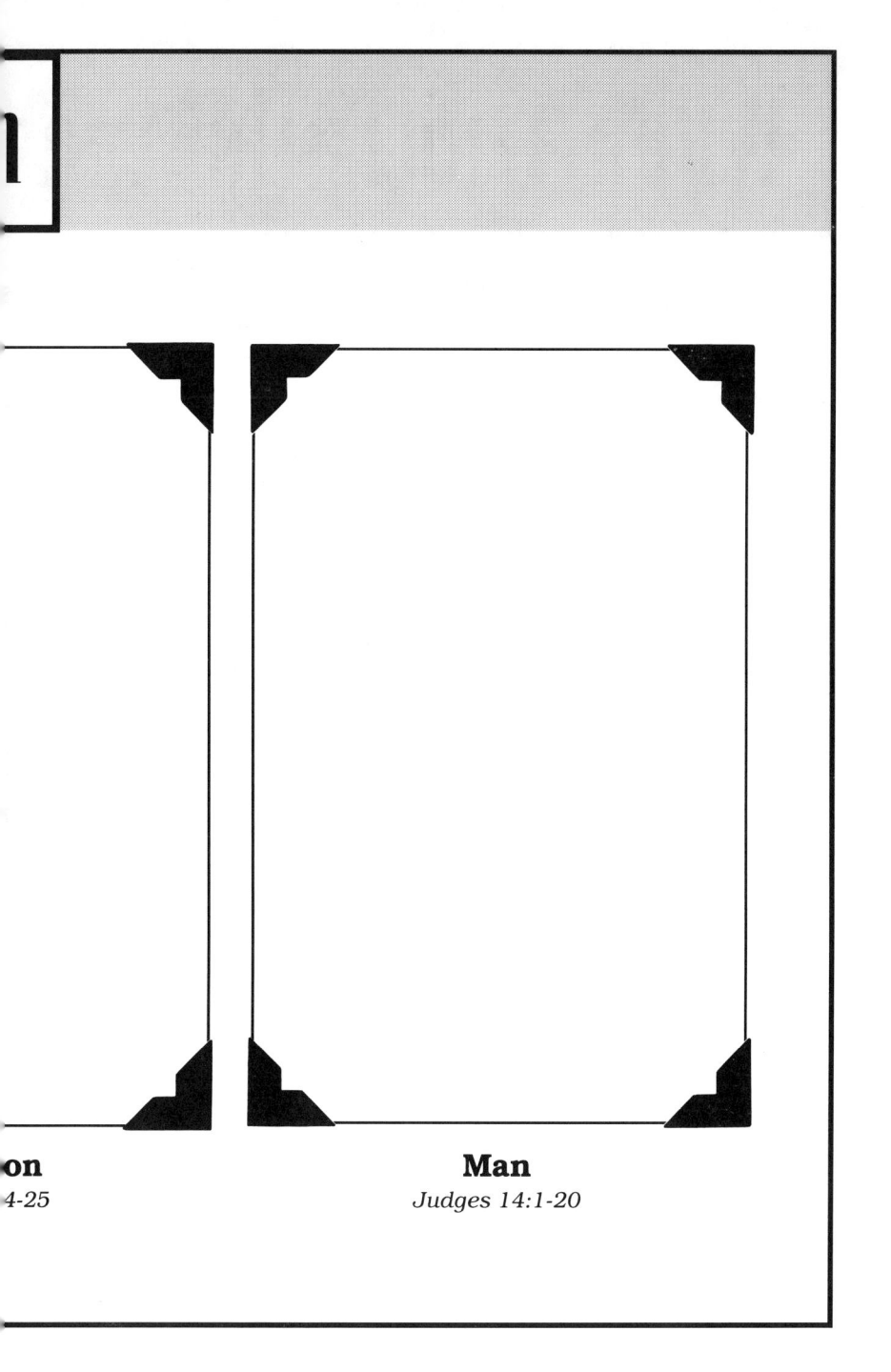

When Life Falls Apart

	Sins
Home *Judges 17:1-6*	
Ministry *Judges 17:7-13*	
Society *Judges 18:1-31*	

Response Sheet 8 Use with session 11 of *Be Available*.
© 1994 by SP Publications, Inc. Permission granted to purchaser to reproduce this Response Sh

Parallels Today	Ways to Counteract

Samson's Family Albu[m]

Child
Judges 13:1-23

Cha[
Judge

Response Sheet 7 Use with session 9 of *Be Available*.
© 1994 by SP Publications, Inc. Permission granted to purchaser to reproduce this Response Shee[t]

itary/Work Life	Jephthah's Spiritual Life
rk Life	My Spiritual Life

God's Prescription for Pride

Read the following verses: Proverbs 18:12; Matthew 11:28-30; 23:11-12; Philippians 2:3-4; Colossians 3:12; James 4:6-10; and 1 Peter 5:5-6. Summarize their teachings as God's prescription for pride on the form below.

SPIRITUAL FAMILY PRACTICE CENTER

HEAVEN
PHONE: 1PR-AYER

GOD THE FATHER, M.D.
JESUS CHRIST, M.D.
HOLY SPIRIT, M.D.

Date _____

Response Sheet 5 Use with session 6 of *Be Available*.
© 1994 by SP Publications, Inc. Permission granted to purchaser to reproduce this Response She

Believers Today	**Me**

Trustometer

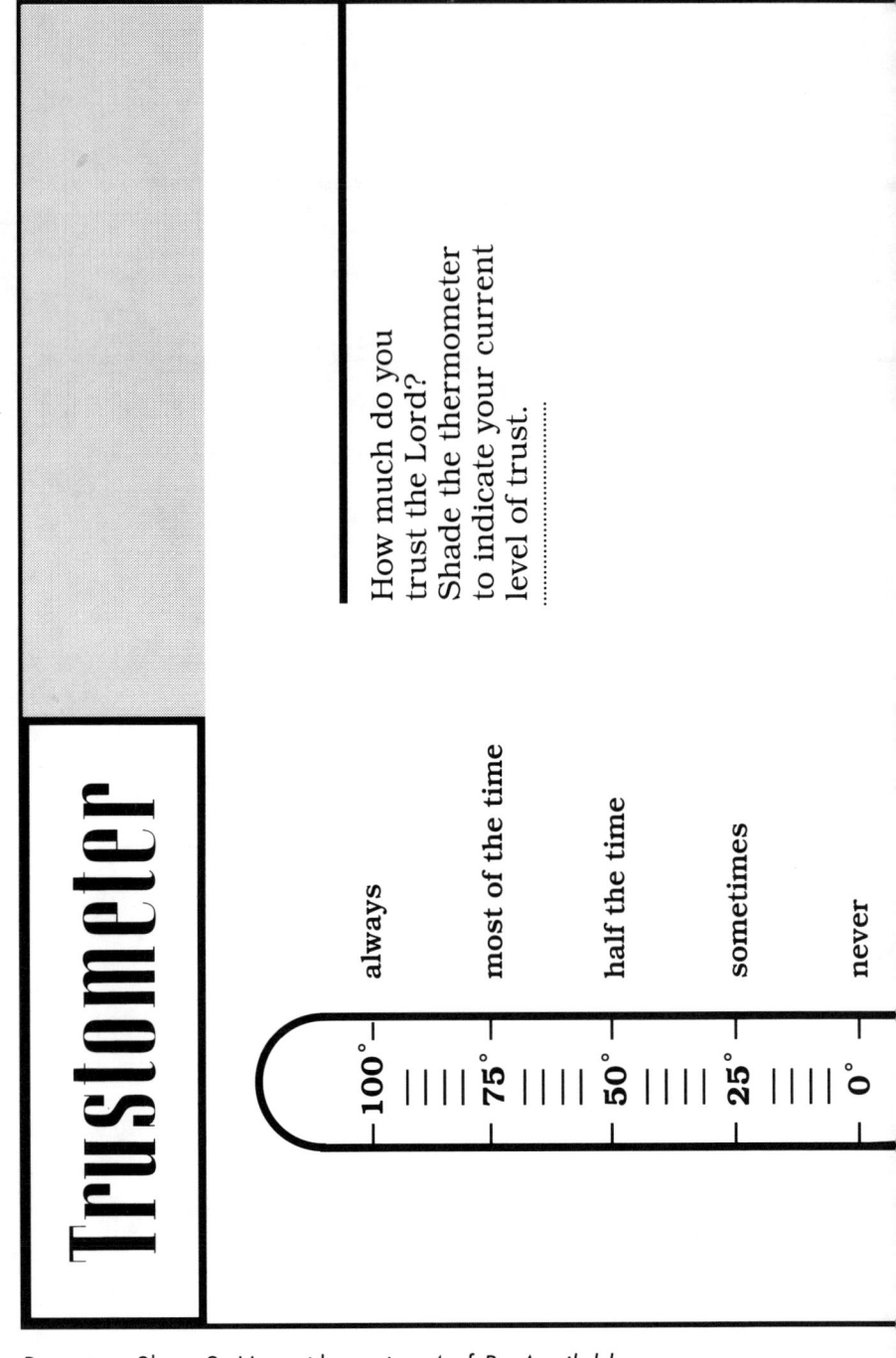

- 100° — always
- 75° — most of the time
- 50° — half the time
- 25° — sometimes
- 0° — never

How much do you trust the Lord? Shade the thermometer to indicate your current level of trust.

Response Sheet 3   Use with session 4 of *Be Available*.
© 1994 by SP Publications, Inc. Permission granted to purchaser to reproduce this Response She

Ehud	Shamgar

Overview of Judges

Theme: Obedience bring's God's blessing; disobedience b
Key Verse: "In those days Israel had no king; everyone d

Disobedience (Chapters 1–2)	

- Early Victories (1:1-26)
- Repeated Defeats (1:27-36)
- National Apostasy (2:1-15)
- Divine Mercy (2:16-23)
- Othniel, Ehud, Shamgar (3)
- Deborah and Barak (4–5)
- Gideon (6–8)
- Abimelech (9)

Response Sheet 1 Use with session 1 of *Be Available*.
© 1994 by SP Publications, Inc. Permission granted to purchaser to reproduce this Response She

Session Seven

MY KINGDOM COME
Judges 9

TEXT, CHAPTER 7

Session Topic
If we sow disobedience, we will reap destruction and downfall.

Session Goals
1. To identify examples of reaping what is sown.
2. To discover how Abimelech reaped what he sowed.
3. To identify ways we think we can disobey and not reap the consequences.
4. To plan ways to root out disobedience in our lives.

Materials Needed
√Bible
√*Be Available*
√Paper and pencils
√Poster board with marking pens
√Visual Sketch 3
√Note cards

Special Preparation
1. Study the Parable of the Soils in Matthew 13:1-23. What do you learn about sowing and reaping from this parable?
2. Read the following verses that deal with sowing and reaping: Job 4:8; Psalm 126:5-6; Proverbs 6:14; 16:28; 22:8; Hosea 8:7; 10:12; Galatians 6:7-9. Add insights from these verses to your teaching or use some of them in your session.
3. Prepare Visual Sketch 3 as a poster.

45

LESSON PLAN

Launching the Lesson   *(5 minutes)*

Ask group members to identify examples of reaping what we sow in a variety of areas, such as agriculture, parenting, and finances.

Point out that Abimelech's life in Judges 9 provides another example of this principle.

Discovering God's Principles   *(25–35 minutes)*

Prepare for a political debate between candidates Abimelech and Jotham. Assign half of the group to play the role of Abimelech and the other half to play Jotham. Tell them to read Judges 9:1-21, focusing on each man's character, his party's platform (what he stands for), and plans to accomplish his goals. Since Jotham was not interested in being king, members who role-play him should focus on exposing Abimelech's weaknesses, presenting an offensive campaign. Give everyone paper and pencils for notes.

After eight to ten minutes, conduct the debate with everyone taking the role of his assigned character. Let the group have fun, but keep them focused on the relevant points in this passage.

Say: **Abimelech did become king, and everything was OK for three years. But then he began to reap what he had sown. What did Abimelech sow in order to become king?**

Have the group read the rest of Judges 9. Then ask: **What did Abimelech reap as a result of what he sowed?** Display Visual Sketch 3 and read Galatians 6:5-10 to reinforce this principle.

"Once we have finished sowing, we cannot change the harvest."
–Warren W. Wiersbe–

Visual Sketch 3
The principle of reaping what we sow is just as evident in our spiritual lives as it is in agriculture.

Applying the Truth *(8–10 minutes)*

Say: **Abimelech thought he could disobey God and get away with it, but he didn't.** Discuss:

- *Do you believe that every act of disobedience to God a has negative consequence for the person who is disobedient? Why or why not?*
- *Give some examples of disobedient acts that might not "reap" negative consequences until long after the disobedience.*
- *Do we reap what we sow even if we are sorry for what we have done? Explain.*
- *What are some specific ways we think we can disobey and get away with it?*
- *What are some possible consequences of those acts of disobedience?*

Have group members think about their own lives and ways they are sowing disobedience. Give everyone a note card. Ask them to write down ways they will root out this disobedience so they won't reap the consequences of it.

Prayer Time *(5 minutes)*

Close with a few minutes of silent prayer. Encourage everyone to talk to God about any disobedience they've tolerated in their lives and to ask for His help to sow obedience instead.

ASSIGNMENT

1. Tell everyone to read Judges 10–12 and chapter 8 of *Be Available* for the next study.
2. Encourage them to memorize Galatians 6:7-9.
3. Have group members watch for stories in the newspaper or magazines or on TV newscasts about people from less than desirable backgrounds who make good or who are seemingly losers and become winners.

Session Eight

LOCAL REJECT MAKES GOOD
Judges 10–12

TEXT, CHAPTER 8

Session Topic
Background is not a handicap to usefulness in God's service.

Session Goals
1. To identify losers who became winners.
2. To explore Jephthah's rise from a bad background to God's choice as a leader.
3. To pray about how God wants to use us in spite of our backgrounds.

Materials Needed
√ Bible
√ *Be Available*
√ Visual Sketch 4
√ Poster of Visual Sketch 1
√ Copies of Response Sheet 6
√ Pencils
√ Chalkboard and chalk (optional)

Special Preparation
1. Study the subject of vows, using an exhaustive concordance or *Nave's Topical Bible.* Concentrate on Ecclesiastes 5:1-6. Prepare to share some of your discoveries when you talk about Jephthah's vow.
2. Pray for each group member by name, asking God to show each one how He wants to use him or her.
3. Prepare Visual Sketch 4 as a poster or plan to draw it on the chalkboard before the session begins.

LESSON PLAN

Building the Body *(5 minutes)*

Ask for reports on the assignment from the last session. **How did you do in dealing with disobedience in your life? How has Galatians 6:7-9 helped you this week?**

Launching the Lesson *(5 minutes)*

Show Visual Sketch 4, and ask for examples of losers who became winners, rejected people who were elevated to places of honor or authority. Try to get examples from a variety of arenas, such as literature, sports, politics, history, and the Bible. Point out that today's judge would make this list.

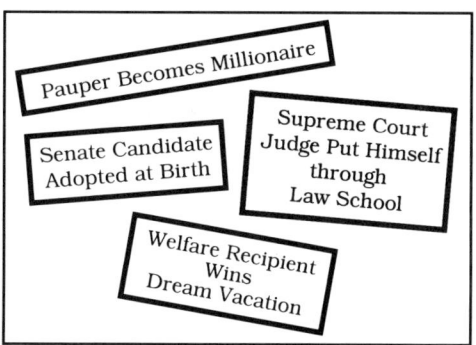

```
   Pauper Becomes Millionaire

                    Supreme Court
  Senate Candidate  Judge Put Himself
  Adopted at Birth       through
                       Law School

         Welfare Recipient
              Wins
          Dream Vacation
```

Visual Sketch 4
Headlines like these illustrate people's interest in losers who become winners. When those who are rejected gain positions of authority or honor, they become news.

Discovering God's Principles *(25–40 minutes)*

Have group members turn to Judges 10. Ask a volunteer to read verses 1 through 5 aloud. Use the following questions to study these two judges:

■ *What kind of judges were Tola and Jair?*

49

- *How did they differ from previous judges?*
- *What impact did they have on Israel?*

Have someone read verses 6-18 aloud. Display the Visual Sketch 1 poster. Identify the steps in this new cycle in Israel's history. Then discuss these questions:

- *Why was Israel attracted to other gods so frequently?*
- *Why are we?*
- *What happens as a result?*
- *How is the lack of adequate leadership part of God's judgment?*

(Optional) Summarize the situation by reading these comments from page 92-93 of the text:

Comfortable living often produces weak character. "Happiness is not the end of life," said Henry Ward Beecher; "character is." But character is built when we make right decisions in life, and those decisions are made on the basis of the things that we value most. Since Israel didn't value the things of God, she ended up destroying her own national character. . . . *The greatest judgment God can send to His people is to let them have their own way and not interfere.*

Ask for contemporary examples of God judging His people by letting them have their own way.

Say: **The deliverer God sent for this cycle was Jephthah. Let's look at his background and character.** Distribute pencils and copies of Response Sheet 6. Have group members work in pairs or small groups to complete the chart from Judges 11. Mention that they will fill in the lower portion later. When they have finished, call for responses. If you have time, record them on the chalkboard.

Ask: **How did Jephthah's background affect his usefulness in God's service? Why?**

Explore Jephthah's vow by discussing these questions:

- *What did Jephthah vow?*
- *What questions does this vow raise?*
- *What did he actually do to keep the promise?*
- *What was Jephthah's attitude toward making this vow?*
- *How does it compare with your attitude when you make a promise to God?*

If you have time, study Judges 12 by asking a volunteer to read verses 1 through 7 aloud. Then identify the Ephraimites' accusation, Jephthah's defense or explanation, and the confrontation between them.

Have someone read verses 8 through 15. Ask:

- *What kind of judges were these three?*
- *How did they differ from previous judges?*
- *What impact did they have on Israel?*

Applying the Truth   (5 minutes)

Summarize: **In spite of Jephthah's background, God used Jephthah to lead His people to victory over the Ammonites and to give them a total of thirty-one years of peace during Jephthah's reign and that of his three successors. How are you like Jephthah?** To find out, have everyone complete the chart on Response Sheet 6 for themselves by summarizing their home lives, work (instead of military) lives, and spiritual lives.

Ask: **How might God want to use you in spite of your background?** Challenge everyone to pray about this question, starting now.

Prayer Time   (3–5 minutes)

Allow a few minutes for group members to ask God for ideas and direction for serving Him.

ASSIGNMENT

1. Ask group members to read Judges 13 and 14 and chapter 9 of *Be Available* before the next session.
2. Encourage them to keep praying about ways they can serve God.
3. Have them think about various ways people react to God's call to serve Him.

Session Nine

THE LIGHT THAT FLICKERED
Judges 13–14

TEXT, CHAPTER 9

Session Topic
When God calls His children to serve Him, He expects complete obedience.

Session Goals
1. To illustrate how people react to God's call.
2. To explore Samson's call for God's service and how he responded.
3. To name sins that get in our way of obeying God's call to serve Him and to select one to avoid this week.

Materials Needed
√ Bible
√ *Be Available*
√ Paper
√ Marking pens
√ Poster of Visual Sketch 1
√ Copies of Response Sheet 7
√ Pencils
√ Visual Sketch 5

Special Preparation
1. Prepare Visual Sketch 5 as a poster.
2. For background on the Nazirite vow, read Numbers 6 and the following commentary on it.

   In the external details of the Nazirite vow God was again seen to use the external symbols to teach the inner basic spiritual truths to His people. . . . Obedience to the outward form without obedience in the heart has always been hypocrisy in the eyes of God. In Old Testament days, no less than at any other time, God was after the heart.

The word *Nazirite* is derived from a Hebrew root meaning "to separate." Clearly the Nazirite vow was one of separation. Any Israelite could make the vow, man or woman. It could be taken at any time (6:2). . . .

The Nazirite vow involved two basic principles:

(1) *The "separation from" principle* (6:3-4). Here, the emphasis was not on the things from which the Nazarite was to separate himself. . . . Rather, there was to be a "separation from" on the basis of priorities and surrenders in life. . . . Because the vine products as a whole were classified under sumptuous living, the Nazirite must be willing to surrender these temporal niceties for a fare of eternal values.

The second part of this vow involved the hair (6:5). . . . [Long hair] would be a public, visible sign that the person had taken this vow, that he was foregoing society's dignity. . . .

The third part of the vow involved provision for an emergency: coming near a dead body (6:6-12). If such a thing happened, even by accident, the Nazirite would bring upon himself ceremonial uncleanness. . . .For such defilement he forfeited his status as under the vow, and he could be reinstated only after fulfilling specified regulations (6:9-12). . . .

(2) *The "separation unto" principle.* This was the positive side of the vow, and was its ultimate purpose in the life of the Israelite. If God appealed to the "separation from," it was because He wanted "separation unto" [Himself]. (Irving L. Jensen, *Numbers: Journey to God's Rest-Land* [Chicago: Moody Press, 1964], 35–37.)

LESSON PLAN

Launching the Lesson *(10 minutes)*

Give everyone a sheet of blank paper and a marking pen. Tell them to draw a simple cartoon of how people react to God's call to serve Him. Emphasize that there is not enough time to include a lot of details or a complex situation. After a few minutes, have everyone show and read their cartoons. If your group is large, have them share in smaller groups.

Say: **Samson, the judge we're studying in this session, was prepared from birth not to react like most (or some) of your cartoons. Let's see why and how well he fulfilled God's expectations for him.**

Discovering God's Principles   *(20–35 minutes)*

Show Visual Sketch 1 poster. Mention that this is the last time Israel goes through this cycle. Have group members read Judges 13:1 and identify the phrases that match the first two steps of the cycle. Point out that the despair step is not mentioned here, but that God prepared a judge to deliver them anyway.

To understand Samson's background and character, distribute copies of Response Sheet 7 and pencils. Divide your group into thirds. Assign one column of Response Sheet 7 to each third. Instruct people to read the verses beneath the picture frames and create word pictures in the frames.

When everyone is finished, ask several people to read their word pictures. Let others add to what is said. Use the following questions at the appropriate times.

- *What was the Nazirite vow? (Have someone read Numbers 6:1-6 aloud.)*
- *What was important about this vow?*
- *What was in Samson's favor as a child?*
- *What was the secret of Samson's legendary strength?*
- *How did Samson break his vow?*
- *How did God use Samson's sins for good? Why would He do so?*

Point out that Samson started out well. Everything was in his favor. But he didn't continue well. Instead, he began a downward slide that ended up in disgrace. Display Visual Sketch 5. One at a time, have volunteers read aloud the following sections of Judges 14. Then discuss together the step Samson took toward his downfall. Record it on the poster with a dark marking pen, and talk about why each step led away from God.

- 14:1-4 (heathen wife)
- 14:5-9 (broken vow)
- 14:10-18 (gambling)
- 14:19-20 (violent anger)

Mention that you will finish these steps next time.

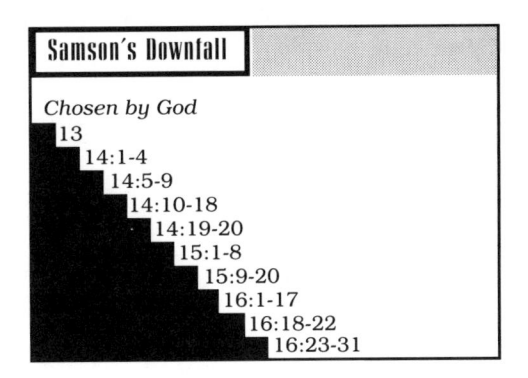

```
| Samson's Downfall |
| Chosen by God
|  13
|    14:1-4
|     14:5-9
|       14:10-18
|         14:19-20
|           15:1-8
|             15:9-20
|               16:1-17
|                 16:18-22
|                   16:23-31
```

Visual Sketch 5
Even though Samson started out as chosen by God before birth, he did not end well. These steps show his downfall into disgrace.

Discuss: **How did Samson differ from previous judges in his call? How did he differ from previous judges in his methods?**

Applying the Truth *(8–10 minutes)*

Point out that God chose Samson before birth to be separated from sin and unto Him. Discuss: **Why didn't Samson fulfill God's goal for him? What got in the way? What gets in our way and keeps us from serving God and doing what He wants us to do?**

Have everyone privately list, on the back of the Response Sheet, sins that they need to avoid in order to do what they know is God's will. Then have them list practical, specific ways they can avoid one of those sins this week.

Prayer Time *(5 minutes)*

Have everyone pair off to pray with a partner. If they feel comfortable doing so, encourage them to share the sin they want to avoid this week. If not, let them pray for each other in more general terms.

ASSIGNMENT

1. Assign Judges 15 and 16 and chapter 10 of *Be Available* as reading for the next session.
2. Encourage group members to pray daily for their partners and to check on each other during the week.
3. Ask them to think about why it's more important to end life well than to begin it well.

Session Ten

THE LIGHT THAT FAILED
Judges 15–16

TEXT, CHAPTER 10

Session Topic
It is more important to end well with God than to begin well with Him.

Session Goals
1. To identify people who started well but did not end well.
2. To discover why Samson's life did not end well.
3. To decide how we want our lives to end and take steps to end well with God.

Materials Needed
√ Bible
√ *Be Available*
√ Visual Sketch 5 poster
√ Marking pen
√ Paper
√ Pencils

Special Preparation
1. Spend extra time in prayer, asking God to show you how well you're doing with Him and whether you are on track for ending well or heading for a downfall. If He shows you areas you need to correct, confess them and begin to take steps to change. If appropriate, share this experience with your group to encourage them to do the same.
2. Using a concordance, read what Scripture says about taking vengeance.

57

LESSON PLAN

Launching the Lesson (5 minutes)

Brainstorm the names of people who began their careers or their walks with God in good ways but then bombed out. Try to name biblical, historical, and contemporary examples.

Point out that Samson belongs with this crowd. God chose him before birth and set him apart in a special way through his Nazirite vow. But Samson didn't end his life well, as you'll discover in this study.

Discovering God's Principles (25–35 minutes)

Display the Visual Sketch 5 poster that you prepared for the previous lesson, and review Samson's life so far. Then complete your review of his downward path by having volunteers read aloud the following sections of Judges 15 and 16. Discuss together each step Samson took toward his downfall, and record it on the poster with a dark marking pen. Talk about why that step led away from God and what we learn about Samson from each situation.

- 15:1-8 (revenge)
- 15:9-20 (bondage)
- 16:1-17 (immorality)
- 16:18-22 (desertion by Lord, enslaved)
- 16:23-31 (death)

Use these discussion questions at the appropriate places:

- *Why was it wrong for Samson to avenge himself with the Philistines? (See Romans 12:19.)*
- *Why didn't the Philistines kill Samson instead of just put him in bonds?*
- *How did God use Samson?*
- *What was the relationship between Samson's hair and his strength?*
- *What was ironic about Samson's becoming a slave of the Philistines?*
- *What was ironic about the Philistines' putting out Samson's eyes?*
- *What do you learn from Samson's final prayer?*

Discuss these summary questions of Samson's life:

- *What were Samson's strengths?*
- *God included Samson in His listing of men and women of faith in Hebrews 11. Why?*
- *Why did Samson waste His life with sin instead of obeying God?*
- *What were the results of Samson's violating his Nazirite vow?*
- *What lessons can we learn from Samson's life and death?*
- *What did Samson learn about God?*

Summarize with this quote from page 116 of *Be Available:* "The life of Samson illustrates the ancient truth that a good beginning doesn't guarantee a good ending."

Applying the Truth (10–15 minutes)

Have someone read Ecclesiastes 7:8a aloud. Discuss why this statement is true. Then ask rhetorically: **How do you want your life to end? What do you want people to remember about you?** Distribute paper and pencils. Have everyone write a one-paragraph eulogy they would like someone to give at their funerals. Ask a few volunteers to read theirs aloud.

Ask: **What can you do this week to become this kind of person?** Have group members list a few suggestions beneath their eulogies.

Prayer Time (5 minutes)

Close with sentence prayers, talking to God about the kind of people you want to be when your life is over. Ask someone to end the prayer time after a few minutes.

ASSIGNMENT
---

1. Instruct group members to read Judges 17–18 and chapter 11 of *Be Available* before the next session.
2. Encourage everyone to read their eulogies once a day this week and to follow through on the action steps they recorded.

Session Eleven

"THE CENTER CANNOT HOLD"
Judges 17–18

TEXT, CHAPTER 11

Session Topic
God's power is the only hope for holding together the home, ministry, and society.

Session Goals
1. To illustrate things that could easily become idols in our lives.
2. To explore why the areas of home, ministry, and society fell apart in the days of the judges and to identify parallels today.
3. To identify ways to counteract sin through God's power in these areas and commit to taking one action this week.

Materials Needed
√ Bible
√ *Be Available*
√ Paper
√ Marking pens
√ Copies of Response Sheet 8
√ Pencils
√ Chalkboard and chalk
√ Visual Sketch 6

Special Preparation
1. Using *The Thompson Chain-Reference Bible* or *Nave's Topical Bible,* study how each member of the Godhead demonstrates His power.
2. Brainstorm specific ways God can show His power today, especially through believers.
3. Prepare Visual Sketch 6 as a poster.

| LESSON PLAN |

Launching the Lesson (8–10 minutes)

Give everyone a sheet of paper and a marking pen. Instruct them to draw a picture of something or someone that could easily become an idol or god in their lives. After a few minutes, have volunteers show their pictures. Be sure that you participate too.

Point out that it is easy to let things like these become more important than God. The same was true in the days of the judges.

Discovering God's Principles (20–30 minutes)

Point out that the last five chapters of the Book of Judges form an appendix to the cycles of Israel's history and are not in chronological order. The author gathered a number of events that happened earlier and grouped them together to emphasize how evil the people had become.

To study some of those evils, complete the first two columns of the chart on Response Sheet 8. Distribute copies of this sheet and pencils. Have group members work together or individually to record the sins and parallels today in the areas of home, ministry, and society. To save time, you may want to divide the chapters among your members. As they work, copy this chart on the chalkboard.

When group members are finished, call for responses. Write them on the chalkboard as they are given. Then discuss the following questions:

- *Obviously these people were religious. What characterizes merely religious people as opposed to true children of God?*
- *Why is it important that each of these three areas be centered in God?*
- *How does each affect the other two?*
- *What other areas of life do they affect? How?*

Applying the Truth (10–12 minutes)

Point out that the only way to keep these areas of life centered in God is through His power. Ask: **How can we make a difference in each of these areas through God's power?** Have group members discuss with their neighbors specific, practical ways and record them in the third column of the Response Sheet chart.

After a few minutes, ask for responses. Encourage everyone to add to their lists on the Response Sheet. Then have them choose one way they can counteract sin this week and circle it.

Prayer Time *(5 minutes)*

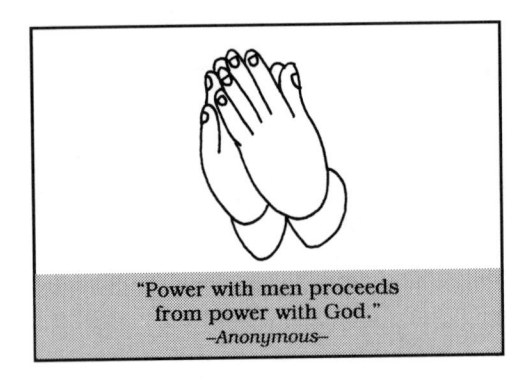

"Power with men proceeds from power with God."
–Anonymous–

Visual Sketch 6
The only way to keep life centered in God is to tap into His power through prayer and obedience.

Begin your prayer time by pointing out the poster you prepared illustrating Visual Sketch 6. After your group has had time to consider its impact, close the session with sentence prayers. Encourage everyone to commit themselves to doing what they circled on their sheets and to ask God to demonstrate His power through them this week. Ask a volunteer to end the prayer time.

ASSIGNMENT

1. Assign Judges 19–21 and chapter 12 of *Be Available* as reading for the next session.
2. Suggest that everyone call at least one group member this week to encourage that person to follow through on his or her commitment and to pray together.

Session Twelve

WAR AND PEACE
Judges 19–21

TEXT, CHAPTER 12

Session Topic
When evil isn't dealt with properly, it has a tendency to grow.

Session Goals
1. To simulate one evil of the Israelites in the times of the judges.
2. To discover how evil results in more evil.
3. To identify ways to stop the growth of evil.
4. To confess evil in our lives and ask for God's forgiveness.

Materials Needed
√ Bible
√ *Be Available*
√ Bags with pictures of body parts
√ Paper
√ Pencils
√ Chalkboard and chalk
√ Slips of paper with Scripture references

Special Preparation
1. Locate a large picture of a woman. Glue it onto a sheet of construction paper and cut it into twelve parts. Put each part in a paper lunch bag.
2. Write the following references on separate slips of paper: Job 28:28; Psalm 34:14; Psalm 97:10; Proverbs 4:27; Proverbs 14:16; Romans 12:9; 1 Corinthians 10:6; 1 Thessalonians 5:22; 1 Peter 3:10-12.

LESSON PLAN

Building the Body (5 minutes)

Ask group members to share what happened when they tried to counteract sin in the home, ministry, or society this past week. Encourage any who experienced persecution as a result, noting that God said we should expect it if we are doing what is right (2 Timothy 3:12).

Launching the Lesson (5 minutes)

Distribute the twelve bags with pictures of body parts to twelve group members. Have them open the bags and show what they received. Ask those with the bags to tell how they felt when they found out what was inside. Ask the rest of the group to tell how they felt when they saw these "gifts."

Say: **Body parts are sick gifts to receive. But God's people in the times of the judges had sunk so low spiritually that some one actually sent a body part to each of the twelve tribes. Let's look at the events that led up to this action and the results of it.**

Discovering God's Principles (30–40 minutes)

Form three groups, and appoint leaders. Assign each group one of these chapters in Judges: 19, 20, 21. Distribute paper and pencils. Instruct the groups to read the chapter and record the people and their characters, events, reasons for acting, results, and lessons for today. List these five areas on the chalkboard. When the groups are finished, call for responses. If you have time, list them on the board. If not, at least record lessons for today.

Discuss the following questions:

- *Where did all this evil begin? What is significant about that fact?*
- *What evidences of good do you find in these chapters? What do you learn from these?*
- *Why do you think God included these chapters in Scripture?*
- *What have you learned about the necessity of dealing with evil?*
- *What have you learned about the necessity of obeying God?*
- *What have you learned about the consequences of walking away from God?*

Point out that God tells us how to deal with evil to keep it from spreading. Distribute the slips of paper with references. One at a time, have group members read these verses aloud and summarize what they teach about dealing with evil. Be sure to include what we are to replace evil with as well as the commands in relation to evil. Write responses on the board.

Applying the Truth (5–8 minutes)

Read or recite together the key verse of the book: Judges 21:25.

Ask: **What does it mean to do as we see fit? In what ways do we do what is right in our own eyes? Why?**

Have group members think about what they are doing that is right in their own eyes but not pleasing to God. Encourage them to confess it as sin and ask for God's forgiveness. Allow a couple of minutes of silent prayer for them to do so. Then close with audible prayer, thanking God for the lessons from these chapters and asking for His help to deal with evil in your lives.

ASSIGNMENT

1. Have group members read chapter 13 of *Be Available* and review the Book of Judges.
2. Ask everyone to review the spiritual lessons they learned from this study and prepare to share one next week.

Session Thirteen

LOOKING BACK AND LOOKING AROUND
Judges 1–21

TEXT, CHAPTER 13

Session Topic
Reviewing truths learned from the Book of Judges helps us to evaluate our growth and encourages us to continue to be available to God.

Session Goals
1. To identify lessons learned from this study of Judges.
2. To review what the period of the judges teaches us about God.
3. To affirm one another's ability to serve.
4. To consecrate ourselves to be available to serve God.

Materials Needed
√Bible
√*Be Available*
√3" x 12" strips of white cardboard
√Marking pens
√Sample bumper sticker
√Sheets with statements about God
√Pencils

Special Preparation
1. Read through the Book of Judges again, and review *Be Available.*
2. Reflect on how your life has changed as a result of leading these studies on Judges. What truths were especially helpful or challenging to you? How have you grown spiritually? In what ways are you more sensitive to disobedience?
3. On separate half-sheets of paper, write the first nine truths

about God from the boldface headings in chapter 13 of *Be Available*. Omit the tenth one.

LESSON PLAN

Launching the Lesson (15–20 minutes)

Arrange the chairs in circles of four or five. In the center of each circle, place strips of white cardboard and a box of marking pens in assorted colors. Display your sample bumper sticker on a wall. As group members arrive, direct them to a circle and have each person make a bumper sticker highlighting the most significant lessons from the Book of Judges. Point out your sample. When they are finished, have each person read his or her sticker and tell how that truth helped him or her grow spiritually.

Say: **We've learned much from the Book of Judges. Today we want to review it by focusing on what it teaches about God.**

Discovering God's Principles (20–25 minutes)

Distribute the nine half-sheets of paper with statements about God to pairs, trios, or individuals. Instruct them to record examples of the statement from the Book of Judges. After about 10 minutes, read each statement and call for responses.

Ask: **What other truths did you learn about God from this book? How have these truths changed your concept of God?**

Applying the Truth (5 minutes)

Say: **The final statement Warren Wiersbe made about God in *Be Available* is the fact that God's story isn't finished yet. We are part of His continuing work in history.**

Read the last four paragraphs of the textbook chapter. Ask: **Are you available?** Then remind the group that we don't have to have a lot of abilities for God to use us in His service. Read the text under the first heading on page 150, "God is looking for servants."

Sit in a circle and have each person think of one ability that qualifies the person to his or her as a servant of God. Suggest the qualities of faithfulness, availability, and trust as well as spiritual gifts and talents. Allow a few minutes for group members to think, and encourage them to get ideas from others if they need to. Then ask each person to affirm his or her neighbor in front of the full group (or in smaller groups if time is short) by stating the quality and a specific example of how they have seen that quality in the person's life.

Prayer Time *(5 minutes)*

Encourage group members to consecrate themselves to God to be available for His use. Allow a couple of minutes of silent prayer to do so. Then close with audible prayer, affirming the group's desire to serve God.

Suggest that each group member post his or her bumper sticker in a visible place at home as a reminder to continue to live that truth from the Book of Judges.

NOTES

NOTES

NOTES

NOTES